DARK TOURISM

TOURISM

California

A Paranormal Travelogue

BRIAN CLUNE

SCHIFFER
PUBLISHING

4880 Lower Valley Road · Atglen, PA 19310

Schiffer Books on Related Subjects
West Virginia's Dark Tourism, Tony Urban, ISBN
978-0-7643-5007-8

Interior and cover design by Molly Shields
Type set in Hobeaux Rococeaux / Caecilia LT Pro

Thin Line Set#27 Travel © Keep Calm and Vector
Occultism icons set © Anna Frajtova
Retro realistic square photo card isolated on
    white background © paullos
Ghost icon isolated on black background © Strilets
Courtesy of www.Shutterstock.com

ISBN: 978-0-7643-6411-2
Printed in India

Published by Schiffer Publishing, Ltd.
4880 Lower Valley Road, Atglen, PA 19310
Phone: (610) 593-1777; Fax: (610) 593-2002
Email: Info@schifferbooks.com
Web: www.schifferbooks.com

Information was accurate at time of publication.
Updates will appear in subsequent printings.

ALSO BY THE AUTHOR
Haunted San Pedro
Hollywood Obscura: Death, Murder, and the Paranormal Aftermath
Legends and Lore along California's Highway 395
LIFE Magazine: Worlds Most Haunted Places; Creepy, Ghostly,
    and Notorious Spots
Thinking Outside the Box: Frank Sumption, Creator of the Ghost Box

WITH BOB DAVIS
California's Historic Haunts
Ghosts and Legends of Alcatraz
Ghosts and Legends of Calico
Ghosts of the Queen Mary
Haunted Universal Studios
Haunted Heart of San Diego

This book is dedicated to Dinah Roseberry,
my friend and first editor and the one who had faith
in me. Enjoy your retirement.

I also dedicate this to someone whom I love
(you know who you are), with the hope that we
will have many more years of friendship and
adventures together.

Welcome to Your
DARK TOURISM
Adventure!

THE SITES TO VISIT . . . IF YOU DARE!

GREETINGS, DARK TOURIST!

Back in the 1990s a new form of entertainment appeared: reality television. And with that came paranormal reality TV, whose investigations and accounts of ghost hunters, monsters, and aliens began attracting an ever-growing audience worldwide. Soon these viewers found themselves wondering what it would be like to go on a ghostly adventure of their own (preferably without all the expensive equipment and gear). Likewise, owners and residents of these haunted places quickly realized that visitors wanted a firsthand experience, and they began advertising their eerie offerings. Thus "dark tourism" was born!

This new form of travel benefited both the location and the tourist in ways that neither could have imagined. All of a sudden, locations that had been on the verge of shutting down found a new market that kept their businesses alive, and travelers looking for something different to do had a list of novel adventures to plan for and look forward to.

Today the popularity of sightseeing and visiting sites of paranormal activity—whether spirits, UFOs, or other unexplained phenomena—shows no sign of waning. After many years of this symbiotic relationship, dark tourism is now here to stay. It grows every day as more locations realize the potential of their long-dead inhabitants, while very-much-alive adventurers seek out places to "get their ghost on."

In the pages of this paranormal travel journal, you will discover ten California locations that have a well-documented history of paranormal happenings. A ghoulish **Scare Factor** guide rates the experiences from 1 (spooky fun for all ages) to 5 (not for the faint of heart!), and write-in pages let you record your memories for posterity. Also included are helpful tips and fun factoids, along with pass-the-car-ride trivia and ideas for lodging and food. So get ready to get your ghost on. Your dark tourism adventure awaits!

BEFORE YOU GO

 X

TRAVEL TIP   **DID YOU KNOW?**

For those heading out on your first dark tourism vacation, there are a few things to keep in mind. First is to call ahead to each site. Save yourself a dose of disappointment and verify that the site is open when you wish to visit. It's not uncommon for hours of operation to change or for restrictions to be placed on capacity to ensure the safety of guests and staff.

It's also wise to look for hotels nearby and book early to avoid disappointment. Many of these locations are prime tourist destinations, and accommodations fill up quickly. For an extra bit of fun, try out a haunted hotel as well as other ghostly locations in the area. This book offers recommendations for lodging and food that will make your dark vacation complete.

Another consideration: just how deep down the (dark) rabbit hole do you want to go? For most casual dark tourists, the memory of the experience is enough. But if you're looking to record your adventure for posterity, you may want to invest in some equipment. A good-quality digital recorder and camera are enough for most of us—just bring along lots of batteries. It's not unusual for haunted locations to drain electronics, and there's nothing more frustrating than having your devices go dead in the middle of a good ghost hunt. For more advice on equipping yourself for dark adventures, see "Further Reading" on page 108, and you can track your experiences in the reproducible log sheets on pages 110–111.

Another recommendation is to treat these locations with the respect they deserve. Many are museums and places with a storied past, and both they and the spirits that call them home will appreciate your deference.

One last thing to remember: ghosts don't act on cue. They have their own "lives" to live and may not be on your schedule. Just have fun and enjoy the journey—hopefully the spirits will like your company and grace you with their friendship. Happy ghost hunting!

ALCATRAZ
A Ghostly Prison

The most visited tourist spot in San Francisco is on its way to becoming the number one sightseeing attraction in the entire state of California. So, what makes this dark tourist destination such a favorite paranormal hotspot? Could it be the ghosts that have turned this infamous prison into "Hellcatraz"?

TRAVEL TIP
Alcatraz is so popular that you'll need to book your visit at least six months in advance. And do not miss your boat ride. Your only other option is to swim across the bay like an escapee (and we all know how that ends).

~ SCARE FACTOR ~

ALCATRAZ is one of the most haunted places in the United States, perhaps even the world. In its day, this maximum-security federal penitentiary had its fair share of murders, deaths by suicide, insanity, and escape attempts, and like many prisons around the world, it boasts a bevy of ghosts as well.

One of the better-known spirits that still resides on "the Rock" is that of Al "Scarface" Capone. Serving time for tax evasion, Capone was well into his battle with syphilis when he arrived at Alcatraz. At one point he was attacked and stabbed by another inmate trying to gain prominence within his cellblock. Capone survived, but he isolated himself from then on. One of the places he liked to hide out was the shower room, where he would practice playing his banjo. Capone enjoyed his musical sessions so much that he is still strumming today. Many guests have reported hearing the sound of a banjo while walking through the shower room, asking the tour guides if the music is piped in.

But the shower room is just the start of your paranormal journey through haunted Alcatraz. Once you reach the cell house proper, ghost activity can become intense. In the kitchen and mess area, visitors have reported that former Public Enemy No. 1—Alvin "Creepy" Karpis—continues performing his prison work, cooking for the inmates. Karpis was once a member of the infamous Ma Barker Gang, having met Arthur R. "Doc" Barker while robbing banks. Karpis was sent to Alcatraz after his arrest and conviction for kidnapping the heir to the Hamm's beer fortune. The story goes that Karpis would walk around Alcatraz humming the beer's trademark song and laughing. Guests have reported seeing shadows darting around the closed-off kitchen area and hearing the Hamm's tune being hummed in the darkness.

Another hotbed of prison paranormal activity is in the hospital wing. It was there that Robert Stroud, the "Birdman of Alcatraz," spent most of his time while incarcerated. Guests have reported seeing Stroud in his hospital cell and hearing checkers moving on a board, along with birds chirping. This may be his way of making the afterlife more bearable while haunting his former home. Stroud, who had become a self-taught ornithologist while imprisoned at Leavenworth Federal Penitentiary in Kansas, was no longer allowed to keep birds after being transferred to Alcatraz for his violent behavior.

It would seem that at least one of the inmates has a strange sense of humor—there are reports of the sound of a rubber duck squeaking in the hydrotherapy room. Less funny is the isolation area at the far end of the medical ward (*right*), which seems to harbor a ghost that just

wants to be left alone. It has been known to shove visitors and tell them to "Get out!" If you venture into this area, be careful!

In May 1946, an escape attempt gone wrong resulted in what became known as the Battle of Alcatraz. Two prison guards were killed and fourteen were injured, and three inmates were later found dead in a utility corridor. So violent was this attempt that the US Marines were called in. The soldiers dropped grenades into the cellblock, and so many bullets were fired that holes can still be seen on the side of the prison. The floor where the grenades landed still show signs of the explosions. Inside the utility corridor where the dead inmates were found has become one of the most active areas for paranormal activity at Alcatraz. Strange sounds can be heard, but when you look, nothing can be seen. So prevalent are these noises that a Plexiglas door has been installed so that rangers can see inside without

As you can see, the living quarters of prisoners were designed for punishment, not comfort.

having to keep opening and closing the door. This clear portal also makes it easy for the intrepid dark tourist to view this haunted hotspot.

Perhaps the most haunted place on Alcatraz is isolation cell 14D. The tale says that a prisoner who had been put in this cell for bad behavior began yelling that something with glowing red eyes was trying to kill him. The guards didn't believe him, but when they checked on the man the next morning, they found he had been strangled to death. Three days later, during morning roll call, the guards saw the dead prisoner in line, though he disappeared before they could react. To this day, guests who go into the cell feel as though something sinister is in there with them. Some have said they've been grabbed, been threatened, and seen glowing red eyes.

Other haunted areas include the original Civil War–era Sally Port, the lighthouse, the warden's mansion, the morgue, and what has come to be called the Dungeon. Proceed with caution, but keep your eyes open during your dark-tourist visit to the infamous island of Alcatraz.

DID YOU KNOW?

Alcatraz is connected to an important event in twentieth-century US history. In 1969, the island was occupied by the Indians of All Tribes, a protest group of Native American women, men, and children that hoped to take ownership of the abandoned island and establish a cultural center there. The group was forcibly removed by the US government in 1971, but the occupation remained an important symbol and inspired later civil rights protests by indigenous American Indian groups.

NIGHT CRUISES TO ALCATRAZ

Many people feel that nighttime is the best time to experience this singular island. As with the day tours, tickets for the evening ferry are tough to come by and must be reserved well in advance. Book through the same site listed on page 17.

A decidedly creepy place during the day, Alcatraz takes on an even more sinister aspect after the sun goes down. For that reason, evening tours are extremely popular among the paranormal crowd. These after-dark visits include access to areas not open during the day, a self-guided audio tour, and special lectures and stories told by park rangers about the island and its former residents.

But it's not all eerie, spine-tingling experiences; there is beauty too. Seeing local sights at sunset from this unusual vantage point is especially memorable. Be sure to take in views of the Bay area and Golden Gate Bridge lit up as the sun sets.

Even if paranormal events are lacking, activity of another type will make the trip worthwhile. Island residents of the avian type return in large numbers in the evening. Alcatraz, which comes from the from the Spanish word *alcatraces*, meaning "sea-birds," is a major nesting site for gulls, cormorants, herons, snowy egrets, and other waterbirds. Having deserted the site during the decades of human habitation, the bird populations have steadily increased since the cellhouse closed in 1963. So channel your inner Birdman and enjoy this special animal habitat and the surrounding ecosystem.

WATERBIRDS OF ALCATRAZ
The National Park Service offers a free online brochure with information and a map of nesting sites. Parts of the island are closed during breeding season, from February to September.
nps.gov/alca/learn/nature/loader.cfm?cs-Module=security/getfile&PageID=388749

TRAVEL DETAILS

ALCATRAZ CRUISES
Landing Pier 33
San Francisco, CA 94111
(415) 981-7652
alcatrazcruises.com

STAY

QUEEN ANNE HOTEL
1590 Sutter St.
San Francisco CA 94109
(415) 441-2828
queenanne.com

San Francisco is a fascinating and haunted city, so consider planning an entire dark vacation here. If you need a place to stay while visiting Alcatraz, try the **Queen Anne Hotel**. With its Victorian charm and elegance, this historic hotel is just what the dark tourist needs for a spirited night's rest.

TRAVELOGUE NOTES

The scariest thing we experienced at Alcatraz was

....

....

....

....

....

Checklist of Frights and Sights

☐ A SHOVE IN THE MEDICAL WARD

☐ A SQUEAKY RUBBER DUCKY

☐ GLOWING RED EYES

☐ CRYING AND MOANING

☐ BANJO MUSIC IN THE SHOWERS

☐ HUMMING OF THE OLD HAMM'S BEER JINGLE

THE ONLY TRUE ESCAPE FROM ALCATRAZ

Ghosts aren't the only surprising things you can experience while visiting Alcatraz, although the Rock's other residents are a bit more "alive"—plants!

Often overlooked by visitors are the 4.5 acres of gardens that dot the inhospitable landscape. These areas of hope in a place of despair were first begun by US military families in the later 1800s, when the island served as a fort and military prison. Soil was brought over and residents planted cottage-style gardens near their homes. These green spaces were continued and expanded when the fortress became a federal maximum-security prison in the 1930s, thanks to a special vocational program for inmates. Gardens are found throughout the 22 acres—around the officers' quarters, along the main road, and by the cell house and recreation area.

One especially beautiful scene is the swath of spectacular pink-flowering ice plants (*Drosanthemum*) that blankets the south side of the island, facing the city, which were planted as part of a beautification project in the 1920s. Another very special plant, uncovered in 1989 near the warden's house, is the rare deep-red climbing hybrid tea rose cultivar called 'Bardou Job', now known as the Alcatraz Rose. These and other species that are well adapted to the harsh environment survived the years of neglect after the prison's closure in 1963.

Prisoners chosen for the program were allowed out of their dismal 5-by-9-foot cells to maintain the gardens, and some even started their own plantings near the cell house, always under the watchful eye of guards in the towers. These lucky men were the only ones to ever truly escape Alcatraz, at least for a little while.

Restoration of the military and prison gardens of Alcatraz Island began in 2003 and continues today. But now it's volunteers rather than convicted bank robbers, mobsters, and gangsters who do the dirty work.

ALCATRAZ HISTORIC GARDENS PROJECT
Alcatrazgardens.org
Free docent tours on Friday and Sunday mornings

Spirits of the
USS HORNET

From the pilot's ward room to the hangar deck bridge to the medical ward, the *Hornet* has its share of dedicated, helpful spirits ready to show the dark tourist what it was like to serve aboard one of the United States' greatest aircraft carriers.

TRAVEL TIP

Inquire about the History and Mystery tour for after-hours paranormal explorations, when the ship is illuminated in red lights used for "night ops." Best for adults and older children (those under 12 are not permitted for safety reasons).

SCARE

THE KEEL for the USS *Hornet* (CV-12) was laid in August 1942. This Essex-class carrier was originally named *Kearsarge*, but when the original *Hornet* (CV-8) was sunk at the Battle of Santa Cruz, the name was changed to honor the carrier that launched the famous Doolittle raid. The vessel underwent numerous modifications, participated in the Vietnam War, and was the carrier that picked up the crew of Apollo 11 after their historic flight and walk on the moon. With a career as stellar as this, is it any wonder that its crew might still be walking the decks, manning their stations and keeping this vessel shipshape long after their deaths?

Reports of ghostly activity began when the *Hornet* first underwent restoration as a museum ship. Workers would hear the sounds of hatchways slamming in areas that were empty or off-limits. Tools would go missing, only to show up hours later in places that hadn't been worked on in months or were yet to be restored. Workers walking down passageways would see items falling off shelves or objects sliding along the deck as if being pushed. As restoration continued, workers began to glimpse figures appearing in passageways and rooms. The visions were fleeting, but everyone who saw these figures said they looked like sailors engaged in normal shipboard tasks. One construction foreman reported that it was almost as if the restoration was causing the *Hornet* to come back to life— and bringing its dead crew back with it.

After the restoration was complete and CV-12 opened for tours, the volunteer crew began seeing and hearing spirits too. One heard what sounded like men working on an aircraft in the hangar deck; the voices were talking about how long it would take to get the plane back into the air and "give the enemy hell." Other crew members walking through the bunk

A mockup of Apollo 11 and the Airstream
used by the returning astronauts.

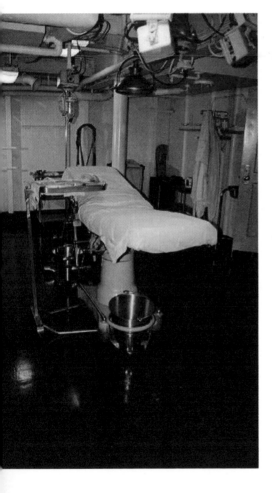

areas have heard spirits talking quietly. Their bedside conversations concerned girlfriends back home, what they hoped to do after the war, and how they looked forward to getting back to their mother's cooking. Of course, when the volunteers try to see who's talking, no one is ever there.

The medical/hospital bay (*left*) is one of the ship's most haunted areas. Many people who take a tour claim to hear the sound of doctors and nurses performing surgery, asking for instruments or bandages, or sometimes even calling the patient's time of death.

Next to the medical ward is a bunk area that is used for group sleepovers. Scouts and school groups can book these overnight stays, and often the berthing area next to the ward is used as well. Overnight visitors have woken to strange noises: the sound of men moaning in pain, others calling out for help, and medical instruments in use. Whispered conversations from the hospital area have been heard by those sleeping near the hatch leading to the bay. Another strange occurrence in the berthing area: on more than one occasion, guests have woken up to find their shoes missing. Their footwear is usually found nearby, although sometimes the missing shoes have been found as far away as the flight deck.

In the forward section of the ship is the auxiliary bridge. It is located just below the flight deck and at the extreme prow of the carrier. Those touring the rope locker just below have reported seeing a sharp-dressed naval officer walking from the auxiliary bridge across the deck and beginning to descend the ladder to the rope locker. The guests will follow the officer's progress only to find that he fades from view a short way down. Since this apparition repeats the sequence each time, it is believed to be a residual haunting, a recurring event that plays over and over in the same way at the same time, and then rewinding like a video to show the same scene again. Keep an eye out.

Perhaps the most amazing paranormal report coming from the USS *Hornet* has to do with a spirit that many believe is a former captain of the

DID YOU KNOW?

Officially known as the USS Hornet Sea, Air & Space Museum, this National Historic Landmark offers a range of fun, interactive programs in the areas of science, technology, engineering, and math (STEM); space exploration; and naval history. Be sure to check out the collection of historic aircraft on the hangar and flight decks.

ship. There have been numerous reports of a man dressed in a naval officer's uniform who stands on the bridge and teaches guests about life on an aircraft carrier, what it was like during the wars the ship participated in, and the thrill of watching the aircraft launched and pride in seeing them return. This officer has been known to take children under his wing, looking after them if their parents are distracted or if the child has darted ahead. Many times, the children's parents have asked managers to thank the docent for his knowledge, patience, and dedication to teaching them about life at sea. The volunteers used to say that the *Hornet* had no docents working in that capacity. Now, however, they just smile and say thank you, assuring visitors that they will pass along the message.

TRAVEL DETAILS

USS HORNET SEA, AIR & SPACE MUSEUM
Pier 3 Alameda Point
Alameda, CA 94501
(510) 521-8448
uss-hornet.org

DINE AND DO

SWELL BAR
1539 Lincoln Ave.
Alameda, CA 94501
(510) 522-6263
swellbarca.com

If you're spending the night aboard the USS *Hornet*, your cot and food are already taken care of. But if you feel the need for a bit of nightlife, try **Swell Bar** in Alameda. Said to have the best Bloody Marys this side of the Mississippi River, the pub offers pool tables and dartboards to test the dark tourist's gamesmanship.

TRAVELOGUE NOTES

The scariest thing we experienced on the USS *Hornet* was

....

....

....

....

....

Checklist of Frights and Sights

☐ *A SHARP-DRESSED OFFICER*

☐ *CLANKING MEDICAL EQUIPMENT*

☐ *CRIES FOR HELP*

☐ *MOANS OF PAIN*

☐ *MISSING FOOTWEAR (WHERE DID YOU FIND IT?)*

☐ *WARTIME CONVERSATIONS*

USS HORNET AND THE APOLLO PROGRAM

After participating in the Pacific theater of World War II as part of the Fast Carrier Task Force, the USS *Hornet* aircraft carrier capped off its distinguished career by serving as the primary recovery ship (PRS) for the Apollo 11 and Apollo 12 space missions in July 1969.

The Apollo 11 astronauts—Neil Armstrong, Buzz Aldrin, and Michael Collins—were surely happy to see the USS *Hornet* on July 24, 1969, after their command module *Columbia* splashed down in the Pacific Ocean, 900 miles southwest of Hawaii. The men were part of the crewed spaceflight mission that first landed humans on the moon.

After *Hornet* picked up the three astronauts, they were transferred to the mobile quarantine facility on board, where they would spend the rest of the 21 days of their quarantine.

In November of that same year, *Hornet* recovered the astronaunts of the Apollo 12 mission, which also splashed down in the Pacific Ocean.

THE SPACE RACE: APOLLO SPLASHDOWN

This permanent exhibition at the USS Hornet Sea, Air & Space Museum features artifacts from the time of *Hornet*'s service during this key moment in US history.

Included are memorabilia from the period, participant biographies, and the mission's command modules.
uss-hornet.org/history/splashdown

Spirits of
LA PURÍSIMA MISSION

From long-deceased Spanish soldiers still guarding the jail to phantom voices heard within the chapel and living quarters, La Purísima Concepción is one place the intrepid dark tourist should make it their mission to visit.

TRAVEL TIP

La Purísima Mission is part of the California state park system. It encompasses 2,000 acres and offers more than 25 miles of hiking trails. Both self-guided and guided tours of the mission are available.

~ SCARE ~
FACTOR

FOUNDED BY the Franciscans in 1787 on Chumash land, La Purísima originally covered nearly 300,000 acres, with a church, shops, houses, gardens, and thousands of livestock for the Spanish settlers and their converts. The settlement was completely destroyed in 1812 by a series of earthquakes that struck the area, and the mission was rebuilt on the opposite side of the Santa Inez River. Today it is part of La Purísima Mission State Historic Park, which encompasses ten fully restored buildings, including the church, living quarters, and blacksmith shop, giving a glimpse of what life was like in an early 1820s California mission.

As history now acknowledges, the Spanish missionaries were often harsh when converting the local Indian peoples to Christianity. Even the padres had a tendency to treat the Native Americans, in this case the Chumash people, more like slaves than converts. The situation came to a head in 1824, when the Chumash rebelled against Mexico and fighting erupted between the Native population and Mexican troops. The rebellion was put down, with loss of life on both sides. Since that day, ghosts have been reported on the mission grounds and in the buildings. Even the kitchen has a spirit, believed to be that of Don Vincente, who was murdered here in the 1820s.

Padre Mariano Payeras, one of the most revered priests from the time of the missionaries, is buried under the altar in the main church. Payeras has been seen standing near where his body is interred, dressed in the full regalia of the priesthood, as if he is about to begin mass. It is said that those who enter the church with disrespect will be cursed with bad luck until they return and make amends in front of the altar and Padre Payeras. People walking past the church have heard a group in prayer, only to find upon entering that no one is inside. At other times, the sound of signing can be heard as if mass is in full swing, even though the church is devoid of any living soul. In the sacristy behind the altar, people have entered to find a priest preparing for mass. Visitors will walk in, the priest will stop what he is doing to look, and then he'll simply smile and fade from view. No one is sure who this is, but it is believed to be Father Payeras.

Payeras has been glimpsed not only in the sacristy and chapel but also walking along the hallways of the living quarters. He is described as old, wearing white or black monk's robes.

A wooden plaque marks the final resting place of Padre Payeras.

The priest may also be responsible for the bedding in one of the rooms being mussed each morning; this room had been used as the padre's bedroom over the years as well as a guest room (*page 34*). Many of the rangers and docents at La Purísima have reported that when they open the mission for the day, they walk through the room and find that the bed looks as if it has been slept in. They then make the bed, keep an eye on it throughout the day, lock up in the evening, and then find it in disarray again the next morning.

The buildings are not the only places the dark tourist will find ghosts at La Purísima Mission. The cemetery and grounds are said to be haunted as well. Indistinct shapes are often glimpsed in the graveyard, and some believe these to be the spirits of those killed or executed after the uprising. Others think that the misdeeds of the Spanish missionaries and soldiers have

No matter how many times the docents and
rangers at the mission make up this bed,
every morning when they unlock the door to
the room, it appears to have been slept in.

caused shadow people to inhabit the cemetery. Whatever the case may be, keep a sharp eye out here.

The grounds themselves seem to be rife with activity. Many people have heard the sound of flute music coming from the area near the smaller chapel and baptismal font, as well as from the area where the Chumash used to gather for their festivals and celebrations. Many times, the flute will be followed by the sound of drums. The drums will begin as a faint staccato and slowly build to a crescendo. When the music has reached its peak, the sounds of people chanting begins, and oftentimes dancing feet will follow. In one remarkable episode, a visitor ran to the park ranger's office with a story that a group of Native Americans had appeared before her and her kids, dancing in front of a giant bonfire. The woman said that the people were transparent and were gone as quickly as they appeared.

Most activity is of a more mundane nature. Cold spots pop up all over the grounds and buildings, even when outside temperatures are high. Male voices are often heard when no one is near, as is the sound of invisible horses clopping along the road. There have even been reports of spectral pet dogs seen walking along as if on a leash.

DID YOU KNOW?

For millennia, the Chumash people's traditional lands have been located in the central and southern coastal regions of present-day California. The original site of La Purísima Mission was known to the Chumash as Algsacpi. Before the arrival of Spanish settlers, the Native peoples relied on maritime activity. During the mission period and beyond, many Chumash lifeways were lost, and the tribe endured much suffering. For more on this Native American group, see *The Chumash World at European Contact* (2011)

TRAVELOGUE NOTES

The scariest thing we experienced at La Purísima Mission was

....

....

....

....

....

Checklist of Frights and Sights

☐ A SPECTRAL PADRE

☐ RANDOM COLD SPOTS

☐ GALLOPING HORSES

☐ FLUTES AND DRUMS

☐ CHANTING AND DANCING

☐ PHANTOM MASS IN PROGRESS

TRAVEL DETAILS

2295 Purisima Rd.
Lompoc, CA 93436
(805) 733-3713
lapurisimamission.org

STAY

PEA SOUP ANDERSEN'S INN

51 E Hwy 246
Buellton, CA 93427
(805) 688-3216
peasoupandersens.com

Pea Soup Andersen's has been serving up warm comfort food for generations, and **Pea Soup Andersen's Inn**, just down the street from the mission, has been giving guests a warm night's stay for almost as long. Not only are paying guests made comfortable here, but its cadre of ghostly guests feel at home too. It's the perfect place for the dark tourist to lie down to rest.

CALIFORNIA'S MISSIONS ALONG EL CAMINO REAL

The California mission system was created to bring Christianity to the Native peoples of Alta California. El Camino Real, or the King's Highway, is the historic roadway built by the Spanish to link their missions and presidios (military forts). You can travel the roughly 600-mile "royal road," which includes twenty-one missions from California's early history. It is said that all of the missions are haunted, and they share a particular paranormal event: each one has had reports of midnight masses taking place in the chapels, even when none is scheduled. Here are few more highlights.

MISSION BASILICA SAN DIEGO DE ALCALÁ

Built in 1769 near present-day San Diego, this is the earliest mission in the area.

Paranormal activity: It is said that the mission grounds and Presidio Park are haunted by a little white deer. The animal has been seen so often that locals have given it a name: Lucy. There is also a little boy spirit who plays on the grounds and may interact with the living.

MISSION SAN JUAN CAPISTRANO

This mission is world renowned for its annual migration of cliff swallows.

Paranormal activity: This mission may be the most famous of all—and one of the most haunted too. Capistrano is known as a very haunted city, and the mission has several spirits, including Magdalena, a would-be bride who died when the mission collapsed in 1812. There have also been reports of a "faceless" monk and a woman named Matilda, who was a mission housekeeper, as well as a headless soldier of unknown origin.

MISSION SAN BUENAVENTURA

This mission was founded on Easter Sunday 1782 in what is today the city of Ventura.

Paranormal activity: Padre Francisco Uria, who passed away in the early 1800s, loved his cats very much, and they returned his affection as best as cats can. It's said that moments after the padre died, his four felines walked out of his room single file into the chapel and jumped onto the bell rope. They began to swing back and forth until the bell tolled to mark their human's passing. Even today, on quiet nights, the bell can be heard. People have also detected the padding of little paws in the chapel, followed by the mournful wailing of cats.

MISSION SANTA INÉS

Founded in 1804, this mission is only 18 miles from Mission La Purísima, so you can visit both in a single day. A stop in the town of Solvang is also recommended.

Paranormal activity: The Santa Inés Mission is said to have what many call a vampire, who will drink the blood of those who sleep in the chapel, removing their shoes while doing so. Since legend says that vampires are not allowed in the houses of God, this is either a very strong vampire or some other entity altogether.

MISSION SAN ANTONIO DE PADUA

Founded in 1771, this third mission in the system is in such a remote location that it has come to be known as "the mission that time forgot."

Paranormal activity: There are quite a few ghost stories surrounding this mission; chief among them is the sighting of a headless woman who was killed by her jealous husband. She is often seen wandering the grounds, looking for her lover.

BEFORE YOU VISIT

All twenty-one missions are open to the public, but be sure to check ahead for hours and up-to-date information. *californiamissionguide.com*

Ghosts of
SILVER CITY

Tucked away in the mountains outside Los Angeles lies the ghost town of Silver City, the most haunted place in the Kern River valley. The buildings have all been brought here from other locations, and many of them took their dead inhabitants with them. From the old Whiskey Flat jail to the rustic Havilah church, Silver City is one place every dark tourist should visit.

 TRAVEL TIP
As an added bonus, the dark tourist can book a private paranormal investigation of Silver City at a reasonable cost

FOR DECADES, Silver City has been a tourist stop for those boating on Lake Isabella or river rafting on the mighty Kern. The town didn't even exist until 1968, when it was created by Dave and Arvilla Mills. It is made up of buildings saved from surrounding towns in the Kern River valley that were being torn down and modernized. The structures date from the mid-1800s to the early 1900s and have been arranged so that no one would know the town was never a genuine thriving western community.

Although Silver City is a full-fledged tourist stop, it has also become a place where ghost researchers go to hunt. The Apalatea/Burlando House, located on the boardwalk, has been dubbed the sixth most active site for poltergeist activity in the United States. It is definitely one place every dark tourist needs to visit. The house is currently set up to look like an Old West saloon. Arranged around tables are mannequins that resemble "cowboys and Indians" playing cards and drinking (*right*). Many guests have claimed that these figures turn their heads to look at them and, on more than one occasion, have even smiled. The startled guests claim that the mannequins then quickly revert to their inert selves. Other visitors have walked by and heard

DID YOU KNOW?

Silver City City has been featured in several television shows, including *My Ghost Story*, *This Old House*, and the Travel Channel's *Strange World*. The current owner not only talks about the spirits here but also hosts seasonal Lantern Light Ghost Tours (call for information). These events are attended by people from near and far who are seeking

music coming from the bar, even though there are no speakers in town.

The most astonishing poltergeist event that has been reported in the town happened during a night tour. Guests were grouped around the bar listening to the guide talk about the paranormal activity in the house when, quite unexpectedly, bottles rose off the tables and began floating from one table to the next. As this unusual sight was occurring, two of the mannequin heads turned to look at the stunned guests. Most of the visitors believed they were viewing amazing special effects. As soon as they learned the scene was really happening, many abruptly left—never to return.

Another of the haunted buildings is original to the property. It was once used by a woman called "Wormy" Annie Sullivan as a bait shop for fishermen trolling nearby Lake Isabella. Today, people claim that while inside the shop, they hear the distinct sound of someone whispering and knocking on the walls and ceiling. A large looking glass in the back of the room has been dubbed the "vortex mirror" because mysterious figures appear in it. The figures change depending on who sees them; on occasion, they have been known to change just by the viewer looking away and then back again.

Also inside this old bait shop sits a small child's rocking chair. This item was dropped off by someone who said it was possessed. It is a common sight to see this chair rock on its own. Then, as suddenly as the rocking begins, it stops. There is a photo of the gift shop hanging on the wall that shows an eerie, almost mean face staring out of one of the windows, which was taken on a ghost tour. The face peers over the shoulder of a guest sitting on the bench out front. Wormy Annie has also been seen many times looking in the windows at people inside her shop. She appears as a kindly old woman who simply smiles at those who notice her.

The Old Whiskey Flat jail reportedly holds the spirit of a Native American man who had been locked up for theft; he died in a fire that he set trying to keep warm. Over the years, this former inmate has appeared to children, but only as a man who is sleeping. When the children mention the man to their parents, he is still visible to the kids but not the adults. There is also a little girl dressed in pioneer style, who has been photographed many times. No one is sure who she is or why she is in the jail.

Wormy Annie's (*right*) and the Old Baptist Church (*left*) have a long history of paranormal activity.

The Old Baptist church in the town also has its share of occurrences. Many balls of light have been seen with the naked eye. This might not seem like much until you realize that there is no electricity in, or near, the church. One investigator who was filming in the church while running a recorder was told by a spirit, in no uncertain terms, "Stop looking at me!"

The unrestored bunkhouse has a few ghostly ranch hands still hanging around, as well as the spirit of a cowboy who has been seen and heard walking the boardwalks of the town. This may be the same spirit responsible for the experience that some women have had of their hair being stroked and their backs rubbed by unseen hands. It is not unusual for the current owner to see female guests dashing from the town as if startled by something unpleasant or downright frightening.

Silver City Ghost Town may not be what one expects from a traditional abandoned town, but it is as its title implies: a town of ghosts. These spirits came from all over the Kern River valley and from all walks of life (and death). They now reside in this small, out-of-the-way tourist attraction, ready to show the intrepid dark tourist what life was like back in their day.

3829 Lake Isabella Blvd.
Bodfish, CA 93205
(760) 379-5146
ghosttown@verizon.net

STAY

SIERRA GATEWAY COTTAGES
13512 Sierra Way
Kernville, CA 93238
(760) 223-6269
sierragatewaycottages.com

The **Sierra Gateway Cottages** in nearby Kernville is made up of cabins rented in the Airbnb style. Number 5—known as the bunkhouse—is just the place for the dark tourist to stay while hanging out in the beautiful Kern River valley. With a full kitchen, BBQ area, and enough space for a whole dark-tourism group, this is a perfect home away from home for adventurers. Just make sure you cook enough for Bob Hope's nephew. You may not always be able to see him, but he still loves a good cookout, even in death.

TRAVELOGUE NOTES

The scariest thing we experienced in Silver City was

....

....

....

....

....

Checklist of Frights and Sights

☐ "LIVING" MANNEQUINS

☐ FIGURES IN THE "VORTEX MIRROR"

☐ WORMY ANNIE AT HER SHOP WINDOW

☐ KNOCKING ON WALLS AND CEILINGS

☐ FLOATING BOTTLES

☐ HOVERING ORBS OF LIGHT

THE LOST TOWN OF WHISKEY FLAT

Who doesn't love a mysterious underwater town? Located not far from Silver City, the submerged town of Whiskey Flat offers a perfectly unsettling pitstop for the dark tourist on the road.

Like many gold-mining camps that sprung up in California during the late 1840s and 1850s, Whiskey Flat grew quickly and shrunk just as fast with the shift from panning by hand to mining by machine. The town changed names several times in its history and is today most famous for its underwater location, the result of being submerged during the creation of the Lake Isabella reservoir. Although most of the town was moved before being inundated, when the lake's waters recede, some of the buliding ruins can still be seen.

A good time to plan a visit to the area is around mid-February, during Whiskey Flat Days. This four-day festival takes place over the Presidents' Day holiday. Located in nearby Kernville, it offers Old West— themed activities, food, reenactments, and rides for all ages.

whiskeyflatdays.com

CALIFORNIA
Trivia

1. What is California's nickname?
A. the Gold Rush State
B. the Bay State
C. the Golden State

2. What is California's state motto?
A. Eureka!
B. Live free or die!
C. I'll be back.

3. The highest temperature in the world was recorded in California's Death Valley in 1913. What number did the mercury reach?
A. 124°F
B. 134°F
C. 144°F

4. The state flower of California is the _____ .
A. poppy
B. daisy
C. marigold

5. California has the largest population of any US state at _____ .
A. 22 million
B. 33 million
C. 44 million

6. What is California's state tree?
A. the palm tree
B. the redwood tree
C. the avocado tree

7. What sweet treat was invented in California?
A. the Baby Ruth candy bar
B. the ice cream cone
C. the fortune cookie

8. California became the 31st state in what year?
A. 1842
B. 1850
C. 1866

9. What animal appears on the California state flag?
A. an anteater
B. a grizzly bear
C. a groundhog

10. What are the two official ghost towns of California?
A. Keeler and Ballarat
B. Cerro Gordo and Amboy
C. Calico and Bodie

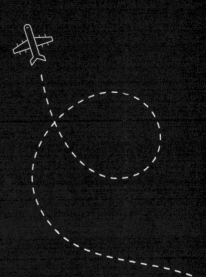

CALICO GHOST TOWN
1881 *Largest silver mining camp in California* 1896

Haunts of
CALICO GHOST TOWN

Calico is not your typical ghost town. It isn't a run-down decaying vestige in the middle of the desert or on the top of a mountain. It's a relic, a real historic silver-mining camp that has been transformed into a museum and tourist attraction thanks to Walter Knott, of Knott's Berry Farm fame. Set between the sprawling city of Los Angeles and the neon lights of Las Vegas, it may also be among the most haunted places in the world.

CALICO sprang up in the 1880s, when silver was found in the hills of the Calico Mountains. Over the next few years, so many miners filed claims that a town rose up amid the seemingly unbuildable terrain. As the town grew and then slowly died, the result of the silver mines finally being played out, a strange thing happened. Even with the extreme heat of the Mojave Desert beating down and with water hard to find, the miners and townsfolk fell in love with the tiny town in the hills. Unfortunately, necessity outweighed affection, and the residents left to find an easier life somewhere else. All but one, that is. Lucy Lane decided to stay.

Well, in truth, many residents stayed on—they were just no longer living.

Walter Knott was one of the people who fell in love with Calico. In the early 1950s, he purchased the town and restored or, as he called it, "de-ghosted" it—bringing the town back to its former glory days. Walter had built a replica of Calico at his amusement park in Buena Park, California. Since he had worked at Calico as a young man, he was eager to show the world what a real Wild West mining town looked like. What neither he nor the County of San Bernardino expected to find was the sheer number of ghosts who still inhabited their old hometown.

One of the most haunted spots in the town is the old Maggie Mine, which today costs $3 to tour (*right*). Even if there is no one in the mine but you, the space feels strangely crowded. Legend says that the gnome-like fairy miners, known as Tommyknockers, are still busy trying to find precious metals. You can hear their hammers busy at work. At the exit of the mine is a stairway that leads to a door. Many people have seen a line of spectral miners descending these steps; they claim that the figures appear to be in various states of decay. In the glory hole and area around it, people have heard the sounds of men working, talking, and sometimes laughing at jokes that only they can hear, even though the guests can clearly see there is no one there. For these reasons, the Maggie Mine is a must-see for the serious dark tourist.

The mine is not the only place where ghosts like to make themselves known. The schoolhouse has become famous as a symbol of the town because of the spectral teacher who still likes to educate those who will listen (*next page*). Guests will ask the rangers about the docent in period dress, telling them how wonderful her performance was. Imagine their shock when they learn that no one works at the school. People have taken pictures with this pleasant spirit only to notice later that the woman has faded from the photo.

Many of the shops in town have a ghost as well. The supernatural resident of the Sweet Shop is a little boy who likes to play jokes on the employees; it's believed that he also pretends to be part of the porch poles at Dorsey's Dog House next door. The Candle and Basket Shop seems to have a female spirit who gets jealous over male customers—and lets the female clerks know about her discontent in no uncertain terms. This spirit has caused glass items to fall from shelves behind the counter when a female clerk is

working, has tossed objects from shelves in the clerk's direction, and has, on more than one occasion, locked the girl in the bathroom. The Calico Print Store across the street has a resident cowboy who gets into moods, and the R&D Fossil Shop is so haunted that the employees and the spirit have actually become friends. The spirit, thought to be Marshal John King, has taken it upon himself to be their protector by alerting the workers of anyone entering the shop. Just don't put Elvis on the radio. John detests "the King" so much that he will either change the station or turn the radio off in a huff.

The eateries at Calico are also not immune to ghostly activity—they all seem to have their own culinary spiritual critics. The Old Miner's Café at the top of town has a spirit that likes to play jokes on the employees by moving things around in the stockroom and tossing buns at the chef while he cooks. Lil's Saloon appears to have a few ghosts who like to play poker and drink beer. And the Calico House Restaurant, the town's only full-service, sit-down eatery, has a spirit that enjoys turning up the volume full blast on the radio and calling out for the employees while they're busy at work in the back.

The town has so many spirits that, on occasion, they have been seen walking the streets in broad daylight or sitting on a bench whittling the time away. One of the town's former character actors is still entertaining children with stories of old Calico. Dorsey, the long-deceased mail-carrying dog, has been seen waiting for his mail pouch, and Lucy Lane, who lived in Calico from 1885 until her death in 1967, has been seen and heard in her old house and spotted walking across the street from the store that she and her husband owned, carrying bags of groceries back home.

There are many more stories that just cannot fit into this small telling, so be sure to experience the town for yourself. With a few haunted sites in nearby Barstow, California, a trip to and stay at Calico Ghost Town can turn into a full dark-tourist vacation.

36600 Ghost Town Rd.
Yermo, CA 92398
(760) 254-1123
parks.sbcounty.gov/park/
calico-ghost-town-
regional-park
For information on
nightly Ghost Tours:
(760) 254-3719

DINE

DINAPOLI'S FIREHOUSE

3158 East Main St.
Barstow, CA 92311
(760) 256-1094
dinapolisfirehouse.com

Walking around a tourist ghost town can certainly work up an appetite. For those wanting a delicious Italian meal after wandering the dusty streets of Calico, **DiNapoli's Firehouse** in nearby Barstow is a must. This restaurant may be the best Italian eatery you will ever find. From lasagna and traditional spaghetti to shrimp scampi and linguini piled high with clams both on and off the shell, the dark tourist can't go wrong. While dining in this fantastic eatery, keep an eye out for otherworldly guests. The staff say that even though DiNapoli's is not haunted, they do get "visited" by spirits. You know a place is good when even the dead come back to dine!

TRAVELOGUE NOTES

The scariest thing we experienced at Calico Ghost Town was

....

....

....

....

....

Checklist of Frights and Sights

☐ *TOMMYKNOCKER HAMMERS*

☐ *A GHOSTLY SCHOOLTEACHER*

☐ *DORSEY THE MAIL DOG*

☐ *OBJECTS FLYING OFF SHELVES*

☐ *SPECTRAL MINERS*

☐ *FLYING BUNS*

GHOST TOWNS OF CALIFORNIA

Calico and Silver City (page 40) are just two of the many ghost towns scattered throughout California that warrant a visit. Some were abandoned because of natural phenomena, such as a loss of a reliable water supply, while others saw their populations disappear when local industries like gold mining went bust. Though not every site boasts paranormal activity, all are a bit creepy and fun dark-tourist destinations.

COLONEL ALLENSWORTH STATE HISTORIC PARK

The town of Allensworth was founded by Allen Allensworth and four other settlers as a place where African Americans could create their own American Dream free from racism and discrimination. Although now mostly abandoned, a group of volunteers works to restore early buildings, including the school, library, Baptist church, and the colonel's home. Now part of the California State Park System, the site is open for visitors and special events.

BODIE STATE HISTORIC PARK

A true California gold-mining ghost town of the 1850s, Bodie once boasted a population of 10,000 but today welcomes only tourists to its many abandoned buildings. Located within a state park, the site contains a museum and visitor center, including restrooms, that are open seasonally.

GOFFS

Founded in 1883 and once a stop on Route 66, this former railroad junction lost its livelihood after the roadway was realigned in 1931. Today visitors can tour its schoolhouse, cemetery, and railroad depot, among other buildings.

GHOST TOWN DRIVING TOUR

The tourist organization Visit California offers a Ghost Town Driving Tour that explores the state's "boom-and-bust heritage." It begins at Shasta State Historic Park and ends at Calico. For more information and a map, visit the website.
visitcalifornia.com/road-trips/ghost-towns

Spirits of
UNIVERSAL STUDIOS HOLLYWOOD

When you hear the words "Universal Studios," you probably think about movies, thrilling rides, and backlot tours of Harry Potter and Hogwarts. What is usually furthest from any tourist's mind is ghosts. But in fact Universal Studios is a very haunted place, indeed.

TRAVEL TIP
Universal Studios is one of the most-visited amusement parks in California. If you dislike large crowds, avoid the holidays, especially the wildly popular Halloween Horror Nights.

EVEN BEFORE you get into the amusement park at Universal, you must walk from the parking structure, through CityWalk, and finally into the long lines of the entrance. CityWalk has its share of ghosts. Just behind the Raiders Store, as you leave the parking lot, is a women's restroom (*right*). It is said that a ghost there likes to open and close the stall doors, making noise to let those using the loo know that "she" is there. People have also reported seeing a phantom that runs down the main walkway in an attempt to flee long-gone officers. This poor soul has been seen by many shop employees when they are closing up for the night. From the haunts of the Hard Rock store to the ghosts serving up great Mexican food at Antojitos (formerly Camacho's), CityWalk delivers some spirited fun.

Once you pass through the gates of Universal Studios Hollywood, you are entering a working movie studio, something the other Universal amusement parks can't offer. So be on the lookout for some of Tinsel Town's long-dead stars. Lucille Ball has been glimpsed walking from the location of her old bungalow dressing room, across the roadway, and over to soundstage 24, where her show *I Love Lucy* was filmed. If you are on the backlot tour, keep your eye out when you pass by this area.

DID YOU KNOW?

Universal Studios Hollywood is also good for celebrity sightings of the alive variety. This is the only Universal theme park where you can see movies being filmed, so keep an eye out. You might just run into your favorite actors and actresses wandering around the park while you're waiting in line or taking a backlot tour.

Soundstage 28 is where the classic 1925 film *Phantom of the Opera* was filmed. The stage has since been torn down to make way for more rides and attractions, but before it was removed, it was common for actors and crew to spot Lon Chaney walking the catwalks and stages while filming was taking place. A section of the amusement park was built on the soundstage's original location, and it is believed that Chaney, along with a few of the old crew who also haunted the soundstage, now help entertain guests in this area. Alfred Hitchcock is said to haunt his old office as well. It's rumored that his ghost caused Steven Spielberg to move out of the office because "Hitch" kept watching over his shoulder.

Another strange haunting that occurs on the usually mundane but fun backlot tour is a spirit hailing from 1915, the

year of the studio's grand opening. Frank Stites was an aviator hired by Carl Laemmle, the owner and creator of Universal Studios, to perform a stunt during opening-day festivities. The event was held over a two-day period, and although Stites was scheduled to perform on the first day, high winds postponed his show to the next. Unfortunately, something went terribly wrong. Stites's plane twisted into a spin, causing the pilot to jump from his stricken aircraft and fall to his death. Since that day, Stites has appeared in the backlot trying to get people's attention—until, that is, a mannequin is placed in the area where he died. But not just any mannequin. It's dressed as a flier from Stites's time period. Keep an eye out for Frank while on the backlot tour.

In the upper lot, on the left as you enter the park, is a souvenir shop called the Universal Studio Store. This huge commercial space sells items ranging from Harry Potter to the Simpsons and everything in between. Fortunately for us, it's also said to be haunted. The store's ghost usually confines itself to employee areas; it likes to block the door from the basement stockroom with heavy items, making it hard for workers to leave.

Another store that seems to have a bit of paranormal activity is Production Central. This shop's spirit enjoys playing jokes on employees as well as guests. One of its favorite pranks is to turn a mannequin backward, away from the entrance. No matter how many times an employee turns it to face the front, the ghost keeps turning it back. Other notable shops with spirits are the Studio Store and Jurassic Outfitters, the ice cream shop,

The original "Psycho" house is near where pilot Frank Stites is said to haunt. Keep an eye on the upstairs window: you just may see Mother looking back at you.

Kwik-E-Mart, and Feature Presentation, where the Harry Potter chocolate toads tend to leap off the shelves.

The stores and tours are not the only places you can find spirits at Universal Studios—a few of the rides have them too. The Simpsons ride is known to have a young girl sometimes seen in cars that are sparsely occupied; she has also been caught on security cameras when the ride is shut down for the evening. The same little girl is thought to be the spirit haunting the Kwik-E-Mart mentioned above. In the lower lot, the Mummy ride has often been shut down because of frightened guests reporting a small boy standing on the rollercoaster tracks as their car barrels toward him. Even though park workers surely know this is a ghost, they must stop the ride and check to make sure no one is there.

Universal's excellent Halloween Horror Nights seem to have real ghosts in their cast. The maze in the lower lot has a spirit "scare actor" that other crew members say is "the best they have ever seen." I guess we know why. Even the long escalator leading from the upper lot down to the lower lot has a spirit that likes to play tag.

Rides, movie magic, Harry Potter, and ghosts. For those looking for a dose of dark tourism, there's no better place than the wonderfully haunted, and extremely fun, Universal Studios Hollywood.

TRAVEL DETAILS

100 Universal City Plaza
Universal City, CA 91608
1-800-864-8377
universalstudioshollywood.com

STAY

SHERATON UNIVERSAL HOTEL
333 Universal Hollywood Drive
Los Angeles, CA 91608
(818) 980-1212
marriott.com/hotels/travel/
bursi-sheraton-universal-
hotel.com

Universal Studios Hollywood is one of those places that even if you could see it all in one day, you really wouldn't want to. With so many hotel choices, where should the dark tourist stay? The **Sheraton Universal Hotel**, of course. With the chain's reputation for excellence and its location within walking distance of the studio, who could ask for more? The best thing is that you might just bump into actor Telly Savalas in the hotel bar. A perfect example of a spirit enjoying spirits.

TRAVELOGUE NOTES

The scariest thing we experienced at Universal Studios Hollywood was

....

....

....

....

....

Checklist of Frights and Sights

☐ *BATHROOM-STALL DOOR RATTLING*

☐ *LEAPING CHOCOLOATE TOADS*

☐ *LONG-DEAD ACTORS*

☐ *FRANK STITES*

☐ *SPECTRAL BOY ON ROLLER-COASTER TRACKS*

☐ *A FLEEING PHANTOM*

GHOSTLY MOVIES

Like the sites in this book, ghost-centric movies run the gamut on the scary scale, from funny and child-friendly to nail-biting and downright terrifying. Here are some to choose from that hit all the genres and fright thresholds. Watch a few before your trip to Universal Stuidos to set the mood.

A Christmas Carol (1951, 1989, and of course the Muppets version from 1992)

Beetlejuice (1988)

Casper (1995)

Candyman (1992)

The Changeling (1980)

Coco (2017)

The Devil's Backbone (2001)

Don't Look Now (1963)

Field of Dreams (1989)

The Fog (1980)

Ghost (1990)

Ghostbusters (1980)

The Haunting (1963)

The Innocents (1961)

Ju-on: The Grudge (2002)

The Others (2001)

The Sixth Sense (1999)

The Shining (1980)

A Tale of Two Sisters (2003)

Ghosts of
DOMINGUEZ ADOBE

This old home sits on what many might call hallowed or blessed ground—it is directly across the parking lot from a priests' retirement home. Given its location, most people might find it hard to believe that the adobe is one of the area's most haunted places, which makes it a stop highly suited for a dark-tourist visit.

TRAVEL TIP
You can book your very own private paranormal investigation of the adobe. Just contact the museum and staff will arrange for you to come after hours for your own ghost hunt—for

THIS ADOBE was once home to Juan Domínguez and his family. When the governor of California, who was an old friend of Juan's, gave him the first land grant, the residence became the center of one of the largest private *ranchos* in California history: Rancho San Pedro. Today, the Dominguez Adobe sits on land owned by the Claretian Missionaries of the Catholic Church and is run as a historical site and museum.

Back in 1846, during the Mexican-American War, a fierce battle was waged on the hills just behind the adobe. This skirmish, known as the Battle of the Old Woman's Gun, was won by Mexican troops, but the death toll was great on both sides. Today, many visitors to the museum talk about hearing the sounds of battle as they walk around the now-pristine grounds. Guests who have picnicked on the grass of the hill have reported hearing gunfire and the screams of men engaged in battle. Others have caught whiffs of gunpowder and witnessed puffs of dust springing from the ground on a windless day, as if dozens of feet were passing beside them while they sit eating their potato salad.

One family swears that they heard horses galloping up the hill; they hurriedly began picking up their belongings in fear they were about to be trampled. Just as quickly as the sound of the approaching cavalry erupted, quiet once again befell the area. Only the birds and the wind through the trees could be heard. Be sure to keep all of this in mind if you decide to picnic or explore

DID YOU KNOW?

Dominguez Rancho Adobe Museum offers two annual family-friendly events that warrant a visit. A reenactment of the Battle of the Old Woman's Gun, held the first weekend in October, is a fantastic way to learn about the area's involvement in the Mexican-American War. The Día de Muertos / Day of the Dead celebration in early November offers live performances, Mexican cuisine, and an artisan market, with the museum providing a place for people to honor their ancestors and loved ones through ofrendas.

the otherwise tranquil surroundings on your visit to the adobe.

Picnickers and guests are not the only ones who have spotted spirits wandering the grounds. Many of the priests living at the retirement retreat across from the ranch house have seen the spirit of a man walking around in the moonlight or tending to the gardens in broad daylight. The priests believe that the spirit is that of Manuel Domínguez. Manuel was the son of Cristóbal Domínguez, who had inherited the *rancho* from his uncle Juan. The reason they believe it is Manuel is because he loved taking care of the garden and making things grow. He enjoyed strolling through the plantings on warm spring and summer evenings and could usually be found there when his responsibilities would allow.

It is believed that the spirit seen in the parlor of the adobe may be that of Manuel Dominguez.

The priests who have seen this spirit say that he is dressed in the attire of a well-to-do rancher in the early 1800s. He slowly meanders along, with a pleasant, serene smile on his face. They say he looks content and at peace. Both priests and guests alike have tried to approach, but the spirit seems to like his solitude. When people get too near, he will just turn, give a warm smile and a friendly nod, and vanish from sight. He will sometimes reappear in another part of the garden if the onlooker is lucky, but most of the time he won't show up again until the garden is empty.

Over the years that the Dominguez Adobe has been open as a museum, paranormal investigators have flocked to the house to see what types of strange and unusual happenings they can uncover. The odd thing is that most of these researchers get only photos of orbs (which many people believe are just dust and bugs) or, on occasion, strange light anomalies. All the good stuff seems to happen to those who visit for the history rather than the ghosts.

After walking through the house, quite a few visitors enter the gift shop asking if the wonderful food they smelled is available to the public. It has become such a common question that the staff now finds the looks of confusion amusing when they respond that the kitchen hasn't been used in years.

The smell of cooking isn't the only sensation experienced inside the old adobe. The sound of children's laughter can sometimes be heard in the room where dolls have been displayed or in the room where there is a diorama from when the first International Aviation Meet was held at the *rancho*. There have also been numerous reports of feeling a strong male presence standing near the fireplace; on occasion, this gentleman has been seen too. His 1800s attire leads most people to believe it is Juan Domínguez himself, keeping tabs on his adobe.

All in all, this historic museum and rancho is a great addition for any dark tourist to include in their Southern California itinerary.

The sounds of children's laughter and play
have been heard emanating from this room.
Could it be the Dominguez children coming
back to play with their dolls?

TRAVEL DETAILS

18127 S. Alameda St. (CA-47)
Compton, CA 90220
(310) 603-0088
dominguezrancho.org

DINE

PHANTOM CARRIAGE BREWERY

18525 S. Main St.
Carson, CA 90248
(310) 538-5834
phantomcarriage.com

After walking through this wonderful museum and strolling the battlefield and gardens that surround the Dominguez Adobe, there's a good chance you've worked up a mighty thirst. The perfect place for a parched dark tourist is nearby **Phantom Carriage Brewery**, which specializes in Belgian-style wild ales. This unique horror-themed pub and grub also serves fine wines, ciders, and beers. The wide selection of potables is perfectly paired with European-inspired cuisine, house-smoked meats, and fermented vegetables. The experience wouldn't be complete without an outdoor movie screen, where nightly terror flicks are enjoyed with good food, friends, and drink—everything the dark tourist needs.

TRAVELOGUE NOTES

The scariest thing we experienced at Dominguez Adobe was

....

....

....

....

....

Checklist of Frights and Sights

☐ *MANUEL STROLLING IN HIS GARDEN*

☐ *BATTLE SOUNDS*

☐ *THE SMELL OF COOKING FOOD*

☐ *SMELL OF GUNPOWDER*

☐ *GALLOPING HORSES*

☐ *CHILDREN'S LAUGHTER*

Ghosts of the
RMS QUEEN MARY

For the last fifty years, the RMS *Queen Mary* has hosted parties and proms in its lavish ballrooms, welcomed tourists to stroll through the luxurious hallways, and invited both the wealthy and less affluent to sleep in the ship's well-appointed rooms. The best part? The many resident ghosts have been as welcoming as the living staff.

TRAVEL TIP
One thing the dark tourist must remember when booking a stay on the *Queen Mary* is that there's not one room that ghosts do not haunt. So you'll never know if the figure in your room is a living person or a long-dead passenger or crew member.

~ SCARE ~
FACTOR

THE RMS QUEEN MARY sailed the Atlantic Ocean for more than thirty years. During World War II, the ship helped bring the Fascist powers to an end and then repatriated numerous American and Canadian soldiers. The mighty vessel brought war brides to their new homes, saw royalty and movie stars walk its decks, and became famous for being the most luxurious ocean liner afloat. When the *Queen Mary* retired, it became a floating museum, art deco monument, Halloween attraction, and hotel.

According to renowned psychic Peter James, the *Queen Mary* harbors more than six hundred spirits who call the vessel home. These spirits are of those who passed away during the war or died due to accidents, sickness, suicide, and even murder. The ghosts seem to be comfortable wandering the decks, residing within the hotel rooms, and even entertaining the many new "passengers." For the dark tourist who wants to find adventure on a floating piece of history, there is no better way than booking a room aboard the "stateliest ship afloat."

One of the best-known spirits aboard the *Queen Mary* is little Jackie Torin. This girl passed away by drowning in the now-gone second-class pool. No record has been found to tell us who this child may be; the Cunard-White Star Line was extremely tight-lipped about deaths that occurred while the ship sailed, and her identity may never be known. The theory, first put forth by this author, is that she was part of the so-called Bride and Baby cruises after World War II, and that she was traveling under her deceased European father's last name. Jackie has been heard in the first-class pool calling out for her mother. She has been known to sing and will interact with guests if she's in the mood for company. Jackie does not remain just in the pool area, however. She has been seen and heard all over the ship and seems to be most talkative in the museum area, back where the second-class pool used to be. Jackie has also been spotted in the hotel corridors, in some of the hotel rooms, and, once, coming down the main stairway of the hotel lobby in full view of guests waiting to check in.

Captain John Treasure Jones was the ship's longest-serving and final captain, and he appears to have decided to keep watch over his charge long after his death. He has been seen and heard in the propeller room in the stern. It's only speculation, but many wonder if he is upset about the hole in the hull that allows guests to view one of the ship's giant propellers. He has also been spotted on the bridge and docking wings and in the rooms one deck down that were once his and the executive officer's cabins. In truth, Captain Jones has been seen in many places inspecting his ship.

The Lady in White is another spirit that has been seen often by many people. Named for the elegant gown that she wears, this spirit is usually found in the Queen's Salon, dancing to music that only she can hear. She likes to dance by herself and fades from view when approached. This woman has also been seen walking on the promenade

DID YOU KNOW?

Built for the transatlantic crossing from Southampton to New York, the *Queen Mary* made its maiden voyage on May 27, 1936. The ship was so fast that the British prime minister used it almost exclusively during World War II; Germany placed a $250,000 bounty on the ship and the Iron Cross Medal to any captain who sank it. It was retired from service in 1967, sailing one last time to its permanent mooring at the

deck, in the isolation ward, and inside the wedding chapel. It is believed by some that she has taken it upon herself to watch over little Jackie; she may also be the spirit known as Sarah, who has become Jackie's companion.

Senior second officer William Stark, who died when he inadvertently drank poison that he thought was gin, has been haunting the ship ever since. Usually found walking along the sundeck or promenade decks, Stark seems to be very antisocial. He is another spirit that simply vanishes if you acknowledge his presence. There is some speculation that he may be a spirit discovered by Bob Davis, who named him "Grumpy." This spirit resides mostly under the stairs in the first-class pool (*left*) and was given the nickname because he likes to growl at people. Since Stark's throat may have been burned by the poison he drank, it is possible he may not be keen on speaking in the afterlife.

John Pedder was an eighteen-year-old crew member who tragically lost his life during a watertight-door drill in the late 1960s. This young

The first-class pool is said to be the most active place on the ship for paranormal events.

man haunts the area in the ship's engine room near watertight door 13, where he is said to have been killed. John likes the ladies and will make himself known to them, but having been brought up proper, he always acts the gentleman.

There are many more spirits aboard the ship, too many to mention here. On your visit to the marvelously haunted *Queen Mary*, keep an eye out as you wander the decks. From the medical isolation ward in the far stern, where the spirits who lost their lives from disease or accidents remain in their beds, to the forward areas where Axis prisoners of war lost their lives in fights and rough seas, the ship is alive with the dead.

1126 Queens Hwy
Long Beach, CA 90802
(562) 453-3511
queenmary.com
For information on the
many ghost tours and
ghost-related activities,
ask the operator.

For the intrepid dark tourist, the *Queen Mary* has it all: a great hotel room, restaurants, and a wonderful bar. There is no need to leave the ship once you arrive. It's the perfect cruise without ever leaving the docks.

TRAVELOGUE NOTES

The scariest thing we experienced aboard the *Queen Mary* was

....

....

....

....

....

Checklist of Frights and Sights

☐ *CAPTAIN JONES*

☐ *VANISHING SPIRIT OF OFFICER STARK*

☐ *A DANCING LADY IN WHITE*

☐ *UNEXPLAINED GROWLING*

☐ *GHOSTLY PRESENCE IN YOUR STATEROOM*

☐ *A SPECTRAL LITTLE GIRL*

CAPTAIN ROSTRON, I PRESUME?

What do you see in this shimmery image? To paranormal investigator Gerald Reynolds, it seems to show the spirit of Captain Arthur Rostron, formerly of the RMS *Mauretania*. Reynolds took the photo in the Mauretania Room of the *Queen Mary* in April 2010. The image appeared in the room's wood paneling and resembles a period photograph of Rostron in civilian dress, wearing a bowler hat. Sir Arthur Henry Rostron had a distinguished career as a seaman, eventually being named Commmodore of the fleet of Cunard cruise line. He is best known as the heroic captain of the *Carpathia*, the ship that saved the surviving passengers of the doomed *Titanic*.

So why would Rostron's ghost find itself aboard another ship? As Reynolds explains on his personal website (paranormalworld ofgsreynolds.com): "My . . . thoughts [are] that since *Mauretania* is no longer around, perhaps the good Captain finds comfort in the surroundings of RMS *Queen Mary* and visits her."

Perhaps he will make himself known to you as well.

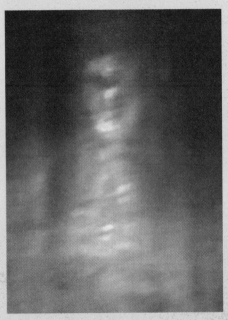

Photo courtesy of Gerald Reynolds

Ghosts of the
WHALEY HOUSE

The Whaley House, in San Diego's Old Town, has the distinct honor of being named an official haunted house by the US Congress. This unassuming property in a bustling tourist district may not look like your typical haunted house—or that it would have any historical interest at all. But this home, which every dark tourist needs to put on their must-see list, has an abundance of both.

DID YOU KNOW?

The myth of the US Congress giving the designation of "most haunted house in America" actually comes from a publicity campaign by the Department of the Interior. While trying to bring exposure to the San Diego area in the early 1900s, a flyer was distributed claiming the Whaley House as a haunted house that people could visit. The story grew with each retelling until Congress was finally given credit for this urban legend.

SCARE FACTOR

THOMAS WHALEY arrived in San Diego in 1851 and built his house on a plot of land that had been used as an execution site, where criminals were hanged to death for their crimes. Unfortunately, pain and sorrow would always rear its ugly head to the Whaley family, beginning with the death of their son Thomas Jr. in 1858, at the age of eighteen months. Later, their daughter Violet, heartbroken over her failed marriage, took her own life in an upstairs bedroom. The Whaley matriarch, Anna, would die in the house in 1913, followed by daughter Francis in 1914. With all this pain and death over the years, along with the executions that took place on the site, it should be no surprise that this is one of the most haunted houses in America.

Almost from the first day that the Whaleys moved in, strange noises and footsteps could be heard in their new house. The family would be sitting in the parlor and have the feeling they were being watched from the archway to the other room. They even heard labored breathing when these feelings came over them.

The archway was once the site of the gallows where James "Yankee Jim" Robinson was hanged while Thomas Whaley looked on (*right*). Robinson's death was particularly gruesome, not least because his crime of stealing a rowboat should not have been an executable offense. Even worse, Robinson tried so hard to keep his footing on the wagon as it was driven away that his neck failed to snap; he then struggled against the noose, slowly strangling to death in front of a horrified crowd. Thomas Whaley repeatedly told friends that he believed Yankee Jim was haunting his home. Even today, Robinson makes himself known in the parlor, and guests have heard his phantom footsteps.

Many people touring the house have reported hearing the sound of a baby crying in the upstairs room that was once the nursery for Thomas Jr. The child died from scarlet fever, which causes a severe sore throat, a rash that can make the skin seem like sandpaper, and extremely painful headaches. It was not a pleasant way to die for anyone, let alone a baby. The pain he must have felt seems to have infused its psychic essence into the nursery, which is why his mournful cries are still heard today.

You don't have to take a tour of the home to spot the matriarch of the family. Anna Whaley has been known to walk the gardens of the property, causing many people to ask the docents about the "reenactor" in period clothing. One tourist reported that she had a nice conversation with this woman, believing her to be an employee. They discussed the importance of family and how people need to cherish each moment. The tourist said that as the woman dressed in period clothing walked away, she slowly vanished before her eyes.

Visitors have also seen Anna looking out one of the upstairs windows, but where she is seen most often is in the downstairs parlor. There, guests have smelled perfume and seen the fleeting figure of a woman moving toward the area that became her bedroom later in life.

Thomas Whaley makes himself known to visitors by way of his cigars. Because the museum has a strict

This archway was built where the gallows that hanged Yankee Jim Robinson once stood.

no-smoking policy, many people find it odd to smell the overwhelming odor of a cigar wafting through the house. Some have claimed that they walked through a cloud of smoke, even though they could not actually see it. Thomas has been spotted on the upstairs landing, wearing his traditional wide-brimmed hat and long coat. He has likewise been glimpsed in the area of the house that was once used as the county courthouse. There, he is known to move objects around as stunned guests try to figure out if someone is playing a joke on them.

Other odd occurrences experienced in the home are the sounds of children's laughter, both in the gardens and the bedrooms upstairs. People have claimed that they see the beds move, as if someone is lying down, and they detect the imprint of a person settle onto the mattress. Perhaps the most disturbing instance of hauntings has to do with people being pushed from one of the steps leading up to the second floor. Many believe this to be an angry Yankee Jim, but no one knows for certain whose spirit it might be. The family pooch also makes an appearance now and again, proving that even after death, dogs are a human's best friend.

With its sheer amount of paranormal activity, the Whaley House can be classified as the most haunted house in America—at least that we know about. For those looking for a place to travel for a bit of haunting fun, the Whaley House, as well as the myriad other haunted locations in Old Town San Diego, perfectly fits the bill. After all, what dark tourist can argue with the US Congress?

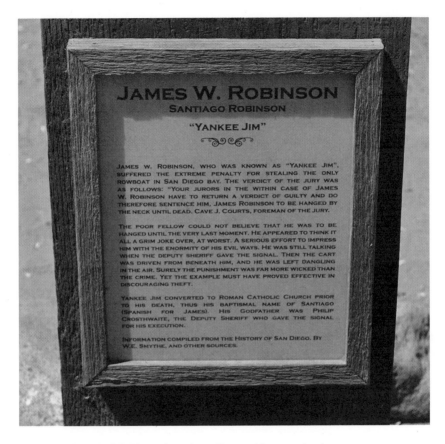

James "Yankee Jim" Robinson is perhaps the most famous ghost haunting the Whaley House. This sign details his punishment "far more wicked than the crime" of stealing the only rowboat in San Diego Bay.

TRAVEL DETAILS

2476 San Diego Ave.
San Diego, CA 92110
(619) 297-7511
soho-1@sohosandiego.org

STAY

COSMOPOLITAN HOTEL

2660 Calhoun St.
San Diego, CA 92110
(619) 297-1874
oldtowncosmopolitan.com

OLD TOWN SALOON

2495 San Diego Ave.
San Diego, CA 92110
(619) 298-2209

Almost all of Old Town San Diego is haunted, and the dark tourist can spend days here exploring and looking for the myriad spirits wandering the streets. A stay at the haunted Cosmopolitan Hotel is a must, and libations at the Old Town Saloon should be on everyone's list. The saloon is directly across the street from the Whaley House, and Thomas Whaley himself is known to frequent the bar, making a drink at the saloon a continuation of the haunted Whaley House experience.

TRAVELOGUE NOTES

The scariest thing we experienced at the Whaley House was

....

....

....

....

....

Checklist of Frights and Sights

☐ *PHANTOM DOG*

☐ *CHILD CRYING*

☐ *SCENT OF PERFUME OR CIGARS*

☐ *LABORED BREATHING*

☐ *ANNA WHALEY IN THE GARDEN*

☐ *A PUSH FROM YANKEE JIM*

Spirits of the
STAR OF INDIA

The *Star of India* began life as the *Euterpe*, a ship thought to be bad luck. Indeed, from the very start of its sailing career in 1863, one might have believed this historic ship to be cursed. With the many accidents and deaths that occurred on board, it's no wonder that the *Star of India* is now a haunted hangout.

 TRAVEL TIP
The *Star of India* offers a program that allows groups to set up private paranormal investigations for a reasonable cost, and staff are not shy about talking to guests about their ghostly crew.

SCARE FACTOR

THIS THREE-MASTED windjammer is the oldest iron-hulled vessel still afloat with a regular sailing schedule. Before its retirement, the *Star of India* carried freight such as lumber, spices, and supplies, as well as passengers. On one voyage, it was struck by a Spanish brig and had to limp into the port of Calcutta. The crew refused to continue with the cruise. Seventeen members were jailed, and the ship continued its sail with only a skeleton crew. On a second trip to India, the ship ran into a strong storm during which two masts ripped away, causing it once again to limp into port. On the return trip, the captain became ill and died. The ship was then sold several times, labeled as "unlucky."

One of the areas that receives the most reports of paranormal activity is the galley. Guests walking along the decks will often smell food cooking. The aroma from the kitchens is so strong and so good that people ask if the galley is open for business. Much to the guests' dismay, the docents explain that no one is cooking on the ship. There have also been reports of pots and pans clanking around. Guests have said they have seen these same pans move as if someone is using them, although no one can be seen. Even when the water is calm in the sheltered San Diego harbor, reports of moving pots have continued.

Another area where the dark tourist might find activity is near the anchor-chain locker. Guests have reported hearing screams from the locker that sound muffled or far away. The voice of a man has been heard calling for help, and cold spots will suddenly develop at the same time as the moans. It's believed that the cries are those of a Chinese crewman killed during one of the ship's cruises. The claxon sounded to raise the anchor, but the man failed to hear the alarm. Not realizing that their mate was still in the chain locker, the crew began raising the anchor. Before the crewman could get out of the way, the anchor chain pinned him in place. As the heavy metal fell onto him, his screams went unheard until they finally stopped; he had been crushed to death. There he lay until the next port, when the anchor was again lowered.

In the officers' quarters, the captain—who passed away on the *Euterpe*'s second voyage—has been seen in his cabin and standing at the chart table. Guests have reported hearing conversations around the dining table even though no one is there. In the doctor's cabin

This doll has been known to watch guests as they tour the cabin areas. Keep a look out, as her eyes may follow you.

and medical bay, people have felt a sudden fear while sensing a deep cold come over them. The medical ward may have residual emotions of fear of death, left over from those sailors who knew their lives were over.

Perhaps the saddest story involving the spirits of the *Star of India* has to do with a young stowaway by the name of John Campbell. John wasn't even a teenager when he hid aboard the ship back in the late 1880s. Rather than having him arrested and sent to hard labor in a penal colony, the captain and crew decided to put the boy to work to pay for his passage. One day, the captain set him to work in the rigging; having fun while so high above the waves, young John lost his hold on the ropes and fell to the deck 100 feet below. He survived the fall but was so badly injured that the doctor declared he wouldn't survive. The crew, having grown fond of the lad, kept him company for three days before he passed away. The captain held a ceremony that all attended as young John Campbell was buried at sea.

After that day, the crew felt that John had never left the ship. After it docked, many members would not return to the haunted vessel. Today, guests and paranormal investigators have reported feeling a small cold hand grab theirs and then slowly swing their clasped hands. Others have suddenly felt cold spots, at the same time hearing the laugh of a young boy nearby. John has also been seen playing on deck or in the rigging. He has even photobombed quite a few unsuspecting guests, who notice him hiding in their photos as if he's following them around on tour.

For those looking for some fun dark tourism, this haunted sailing ship should be near the top of the list. San Diego is well known for offering plenty of haunted activities, and the maritime museum with its *Star of India* is one of the best.

From this rigging high above the deck of the ship, young John Campbell fell and was mortally wounded. The child still plays throughout the ship and is not shy about making his spirit known to guests.

WELCOME ABOARD!

The San Diego Maritime Museum has a few other haunted vessels that are open for tours, such as the 1898 steam ferryboat *Berkeley* and the wonderfully haunted USS *Midway* aircraft carrier.

The **Berkeley** is a must for steamship fans, not to mention ghost fans, and it's where you'll find the maritime museum store. The *Berkeley* has a few spirits aboard, one of which should be given a wide berth. The ghost in question was a passenger who reportedly blew himself up with a vial of nitroglycerin in the men's room. Although it was ruled an accident, his family cried foul play, insisting that he was in fact murdered.

For more inforation, visit *sdmaritime.org/visit/the-ships/steam-ferry-berkeley.*

The **USS Midway Museum** showcases the many accomplishments and firsts achieved by the longest-serving aircraft carrier in US history. Many of the crew who served on board have returned after death to keep this historic ship "alive" for future generations. According to the ship's historian, they have even found evidence that ghostly tourists have been visiting. It would seem that everyone wishes to be a "Top Gun."

For more inforation, visit *midway.org/blog/spirits-of-the-midway.*

TRAVEL DETAILS

Open 9:00 a.m.–8:00 p.m.
daily
1306 Harbor Dr.
San Diego, CA 92101
619-234-9153
sdmaritime.org

DINE

CAFÉ COYOTE

2461 San Diego Ave.
San Diego, CA 92110
(619) 291-4695
cafecoyoteoldtown.com

After a long day, the dark tourist should consider a trip to nearby Old Town San Diego. Here you will find the **Café Coyote** Mexican restaurant, where specters and customers alike enjoy the fine food, great margaritas, and good company. If you see a woman wandering among the tables, or a couple of children dashing into the wall, don't be alarmed—they're regulars here.

TRAVELOGUE NOTES

The scariest thing we experienced aboard the *Star of India* was

....

....

....

....

....

Checklist of Frights and Sights

☐ *THE SMELL OF FOOD COOKING*

☐ *CRIES FOR HELP*

☐ *CREEPY DOLL'S EYES FOLLOWING YOU*

☐ *A GRAB BY A SMALL, COLD HAND*

☐ *BANGING POTS AND PANS*

☐ *A PHOTOBOMBING BOY*

Here Ends Our
DARK TOURIST
Adventure in California!

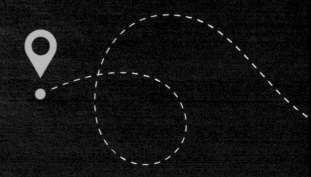

Turn the page for recommended reading and reproducible logbook pages to record your own paranormal experiences throughout the state.

FURTHER READING

Here is a short list of books, for adults and younger readers, on California history and paranormal activity. Be sure to check out the author's other books, listed on the copyright page.

The Big Book of California Ghost Stories by Janice Oberding (2021)

California: A History by Kevin Starr (2007)

California: An American History by John Mack Faragher (2022)

California through Native Eyes: Reclaiming History by William J. Bauer Jr. (2016)

Ghost Hunting Secrets of the Supernatural by the Editors of Ghost Hunting (2021)

Ghost Hunter's Handbook: Supernatural Explorations for Kids by Liza Gardner Walsh (2016)

Spooky California: Tales of Hauntings, Strange Happenings, and Other Local Lore by S. E. Schlosser (2019)

We Are the Land: A History of Native California by Damon B. Akins (2021)

For the beginner dark tourist:
The Everything Ghost Hunting Book: Tips, Tools, and Techniques for Exploring the Supernatural World by Melissa Martin Ellis (2014)

You may want to invest in a logbook—many versions exist online and in books. Or copy pages 110–111 for an easy way to record your dark-tourism adventures at each location.

INDEX

DARK TOURIST LOG

Event ....

Date .... Time ....

Location/Address ....

Description ....

....

....

....

....

Sketch of Ghost or Paranormal Event

....

SCARE FACTOR

Possible Identity or Name: ....

Write a number from 1 to 10 next to the ghost.

Ghostly conversations, unexplained sounds, or strange phenomena:

....

....

....

....

....

....

....

....

Notes

....

....

....

....

....

....

....

ABOUT THE AUTHOR

Brian Clune is a historian and has traveled throughout California, researching its haunted hotspots and historical locations with the goal of bringing knowledge of the paranormal and the wonderful history of the state to those who are interested in learning.

His interest in history has led him to volunteer aboard the USS *Iowa* and at the Fort MacArthur Military Museum and to give lectures at colleges and universities around California. He has been involved with several television shows, including *Ghost Adventures*, *My Ghost Story*, *Dead Files*, and *Ghost Hunters*, and he was the subject in a companion documentary for the movie *Paranormal Asylum*. He has also appeared on local, national, and international radio programs.

Clune lives in Southern California with his loving wife, Terri; his three wonderful children; and, of course, Wandering Wyatt! Watch for Wyatt as you read this book and in others he has written.